"To become a good player, you need talent. To become a great player, you need an attitude like Virat Kohli."

– Indian cricket legend, Sunil Gavaskar

First published in Great Britain 2024 by Red Shed, part of Farshore

An imprint of HarperCollins*Publishers*
1 London Bridge Street, London SE1 9GF
www.farshore.co.uk

HarperCollins*Publishers*
Macken House, 39/40 Mayor Street Upper,
Dublin 1, D01 C9W8

Red Shed is a registered trademark of HarperCollins*Publishers* Ltd.

Copyright © HarperCollins*Publishers* Limited 2024

Cover illustration by Carl Pearce.

ISBN 978 0 00 860888 0
Printed and bound in the UK using 100% Renewable Electricity at CPI Group (UK) Ltd.
001

A CIP catalogue record for this title is available from the British Library.

This book contains FSC™ certified paper and other controlled
sources to ensure responsible forest management.

For more information visit: www.harpercollins.co.uk/green

VIRAT KOHLI

Written by Clive Gifford

RED■
SHED

⭐ CHAPTER 1 ⭐

Quickfire Kohli

18 May 2016

A packed crowd at the M. Chinnaswamy Stadium in the Indian city of Bengaluru were hushed as Sandeep Sharma sprinted in to bowl. Facing was the Royal Challengers Bangalore's captain and star batter, Virat Kohli. It was the first ball of his innings and it was a must-win game for his team.

THWACK!

The ball rocketed off Virat's bat and sped away over the damp grass. A Kings XI Punjab fielder lunged for it, but it had raced past before he'd even completed his dive.

Four!

The home crowd exploded with cheers. Some fans glanced down at their phones to read the text commentary:

Kohli needs no sighters. Stands tall and punches that between cover and point. Shot of a man in the form of his life. Beautiful.

Virat was indeed in great form. He was having a brilliant season in the world's biggest Twenty20 (T20) competition, the Indian Premier League. With just 20 overs for each team, batters scoring hundreds are rare. In fact, in the 2014 IPL, there had been just three centuries in all the 60 games played. Virat in 2016 had already scored three himself, the last coming just four days earlier when he and South African maestro AB de Villiers had scored an incredible 229 between them . . . in just 107 balls. A-maz-ing!

Their RCB teammate, West Indian hard-hitter Chris Gayle, labelled the pair Batman and

Superman, and he should know – Chris held many records for rapid scoring in T20 and ODI cricket and he set off fast at the top of the innings . . . with Virat alongside him.

Torrential rain had shortened the match to just 15 overs (90 balls) per side – not long to build any sort of score. Virat was mindful of this. At least there was a game on, he thought. Rain had washed out a crucial match that stopped RCB from making it to the 2015 IPL (Indian Premier League) final.

Virat had learned how even in a short match, there were times to defend as well as attack. He was famous for his effortless flicks and other leg side shots, but his favourite stroke was the cover drive. "There is no better feeling, especially against the quick bowlers, when you drive them with the full stride, on the rise, with a high elbow," he said in a 2015 interview. And that's what he did in the sixth over, followed by a cheeky reverse sweep for another four the next ball.

"Yes, Virat, YES!" boomed Chris Gayle. The big West Indian liked what he saw.

Virat, though, was wincing in pain. He had suffered an injury whilst fielding in the previous match. Beneath his batting glove just past the '269' tattoo on the back of his left hand (Virat was the 269th Test cricketer to play for India) were eight stitches in the webbing between his thumb and forefinger. The stitches throbbed every time his bat connected with the ball.

But Virat blanked out the pain. Few players could match his intense focus or hunger for runs. He crunched another four and then, in the seventh over, hit a seven! The delivery from KC Cariappa was a no-ball meaning one was added to RCB's total and the ball re-bowled. But the batting side also gain any extra runs the batter strikes and Virat swung hard, launching the ball into the crowd . . . SIX!

Cariappa's next ball was blazed down the ground by Virat for another maximum.

Quickfire Kohli

The crowd were off their feet.

"Six! Six! From King Kohli!"

"Go RCB. Smash them!"

"Kohli, Kohli, Kohli, Kohli!"

Shortly afterwards, Virat raised his bat. He'd reached 50 in just 28 balls. "Surely, I can't get a 100 in 15 overs?" he thought to himself . . . although it would be fun trying.

Virat had joined Royal Challengers Bangalore as a young cricketer in 2008 for the cut-price fee of $30,000 (over £23,600). At an IPL auction today, he would go for millions. Despite offers to join other IPL teams, he had stayed with RCB ever since and had actually played in the very first IPL match, against the Kolkata Knight Riders. There, he'd watched on open-mouthed as Brendon 'Baz' McCullum launched an astonishing assault on his team's bowlers. The New Zealand big hitter pummelled 158 runs in a 20-over game.

Virat loved Baz's aggression, but went on to develop his own T20 game, which included becoming one of the most effective runners between the wickets; he could often turn a likely single into two runs. And Virat mostly played 'proper' cricket shots, using all his experience from Test cricket. So, no scoops and few slogs . . . well, not until the very end of the innings.

That said, he could still play spectacularly. He blasted three massive sixes – over long-on, long-off and midwicket – in the 10th over to reach 69, and then added 24 in the next seven balls as he carved shots all round the ground. He could barely feel the pain in his hand now, and the noise in the crowd grew and grew . . .

"Virat's into the nineties, now."

"Kohhhhhhhliiiiii!"

"He's done it again! SIX!"

"Oh my, that's landed high in the second tier of the stand. That's HUGE!"

Another boundary in the 14th over, this time a four, saw Virat leap with joy. Yes! He had struck his fourth IPL century that season.

He turned towards the RCB team dugout and pumped his fist wildly.

He continued his celebrations by striking the next ball for six (the eighth of his innings) followed by a four which took him to 4,002 IPL runs, the first player to cross the 4,000-mark. When he was out, for 113, the whole ground stood to applaud. Virat's rapid innings had taken just 50 balls and included 48 runs in sixes and 48 runs in fours. WOW!

RCB posted a formidable score of 211 – that's over 14 runs per over. Faced by such an onslaught, the Kings XI Punjabi collapsed. Their whole team only managed to score seven runs more than Virat did by himself!

RCB reached the IPL final but finished runners-up. Virat, however, won the IPL's coveted Orange Cap for the competition's leading run-scorer. He'd driven, pulled, glanced and smashed a total of 973 runs: 125 more than Australian legend David Warner in second place, and with his pal AB de Villiers 286 runs behind, in third.

But those 973 runs were only part of Virat's 2016 story. He also became the first batter to score over 600 runs in Twenty20 internationals (T20i), and smashed 739 runs – including three centuries – in one day internationals (ODIs) for India. As captain of India's Test team throughout 2016, he amassed 1,215 Test runs, including four centuries.

Add all these feats together and you have a truly astonishing total of 3,568 runs in major competitions in 2016. What a year! What a player!

How did Virat Kohli become such a titan of T20s, Tests and ODIs? How was he able to drive himself on, year after year, to stay at the top of cricket in all three formats of the game?

It all started in India's biggest city . . .

★ CHAPTER 2 ★

A Son of Delhi

More than 30 million people live in and around
Delhi and on 5 November 1988, Virat Kohli
became one of them. This giant metropolis is
split into 11 separate districts or territories.
One is New Delhi, which is the capital of the
country and its neighbouring territory, West Delhi.

Split by the Sahibi river, West Delhi is home
to two million people. If you take a short walk
north from the river, through the bustling streets
teeming with people, cars and motorbikes,
you'll find a locality called Paschim Vihar.
There, close to the busy Rohtak Road
expressway, are the Punjabi Bagh Apartments

where the Kohlis lived. This Punjabi Hindu family numbered five: Saroj (mum) and Prem (dad), their daughter, Bhawna, and two sons, Vikas and Virat.

Virat's father, Prem, hadn't always lived in Delhi. He had been born 850 kilometres south in the state of Madhya Pradesh, in a city officially called Murwara, but which is better known as Katni because of its location on the banks of the Katni river. Prem's brother still lives in the old family home, and Prem's sister, Asha Kohli, was elected mayor of Katni. Searching for more opportunities and a better life, Prem made his way to Delhi and became a lawyer and businessman.

A keen cricket fan, Prem was delighted when both his sons started playing – not that his youngest boy needed much encouragement. Virat was only three when he first held a toy bat and asked his father to bowl a soft ball at him again . . . and again . . . and again.

"Another ball. Another!"

"Now, now, Virat. That's enough. I'm tired."

"Vikas, you bowl at your brother. Gently, though."

"Okay, Father."

"Then both of you must wash before dinner."

"Yes, Mother."

Cricket wasn't the only sport Virat fell in love with. By the time he went to the Vishal Bharti Public School, he also enjoyed football. However, like many of his classmates, he mostly played cricket in the playground or in any open spaces they could find after school.

Street or gully cricket might use a wooden packing crate or a stack of bricks as stumps. And instead of an actual hard cricket ball, a tennis ball with wicked bounce would be bowled. Sometimes, a tennis ball would be wound round with insulation or duct tape to make a tapeball, which mimicked a real seaming and swinging cricket ball.

Even at a young age, Virat thirsted for

a challenge. Not content with playing gully cricket with kids of his own age, he often joined Vikas' gang of friends. Vikas was seven years older than Virat but was a good older brother to him . . . well, most of the time. Vikas' friends put up with Vikas' mop-haired younger brother, especially as Virat was a bundle of energy who would happily field wherever he was told to. He just wanted to be involved in the game.

Virat's sharp reactions and timing proved exceptional from a very early age. Like many young gully cricketers, Virat gripped the bat with a very strong bottom hand. This helped him get on top of the ball, which would often rear up sharply after it hit the rock-hard concrete or sun-baked ground they were playing on. Vikas' mates struggled to get him out.

"Your brother is so good at batting, Vikas."

"I know, I know."

"No, he's *too* good for us. It's embarrassing not being able to get a little kid out."

A Son of Delhi

The older boys started leaving the game just as it was Virat's turn to bat. Not fair!

Virat, Vikas and millions of other cricket-mad Indians in the 1990s and early 2000s idolised Sachin Tendulkar. A genius batter, Sachin scored century after century for India in both one day internationals and Test matches. He was unstoppable. Virat followed his every move excitedly on TV and in the news.

"Vikas! Vikas! Wake up! Tendu has scored another century."

"What, Virat? I was . . ."

"*Against* Sri Lanka. 148. That's his fourteenth Test hundred."

"Oh, go away, little brother."

"And his third against Sri Lanka this year."

When sixteen-year-old Sachin started out playing international cricket, he was placed under the wing of an older player, a fast bowler called Atul Wassan. The pair played in the Indian side that won the 1990–91 Asia Cup – a one day international competition. Atul and Sachin even lived together for a time in England, but only on Atul's strict instructions: "I cook, you clean!"

Atul played just four Test matches and nine ODIs for India before injuries stopped him progressing further. He did, though, play cricket for Delhi for 13 years until, in 1998, he decided to retire. One of his Delhi teammates, Rajkumar Sharma, who batted and bowled off-spin, was an aspiring coach. Together, the pair decided to open a new cricket school in West Delhi for children who dreamt of being the 'next Sachin Tendulkar'.

"Father, look at this news."

"Calm down, Virat."

"But, Father, look, it's amazing. *Look*."

"Okay, okay. What is it?"

"The West Delhi Cricket Academy is opening for boys wanting to play cricket better."

"Interesting . . ."

"In Vikaspuri. That's so close to us."

"No, it's more like five or six kilometres

away, Virat."

"Can we go, Father? Please?"

"We'll see, Virat. Better tell Vikas, as well."

On 30 May 1998, Prem Kohli and his two sons travelled the five or so kilometres south to the Saviour Convent School cricket ground in Vikaspuri. It was the opening enrolment day of Atul and Rajkumar's West Delhi Cricket Academy (WDCA). A heatwave had engulfed the whole of India and temperatures were well above a sweltering 40°C. The Kohli boys were just two of 250 young hopefuls, all wishing to receive coaching at the new academy. At the end of the day, Virat was enrolled in the cricket school. His father looked at Coach Rajkumar and spoke earnestly:

"I leave it to you. You are like his father now and must take care of him. Whatever you do will be best for him."

The coach nodded. He knew what Prem Kohli was saying. A coach of young cricketers has a special responsibility – to help the players get the most out of their abilities.

Out in the field and despite the stifling heat, Virat threw himself into the drills and training. He was desperate for his turn in the nets to show off his batting. One of Rajkumar's assistant coaches, Suresh Batra, noted that the little boy with the mop of unruly hair was hyper and cheeky, but also keen and eager to take part. At one point, Virat was stationed out as a fielder closer to the boundary than the stumps. The ball ran to him, he picked it up and threw it hard and fast straight back to the wicketkeeper.

"Wow!" thought Suresh. "A throw like that and he's just nine years old."

It wouldn't be the last time Suresh Batra would be impressed by the young Virat Kohli.

⭐ CHAPTER 3 ⭐

A Lot to Learn

For some children who played at the West Delhi Cricket Academy, cricket was a fun pastime, but for Virat it was a passion. The head coach spotted it almost immediately.

"Within a few days, we could see he was different from the others," said Rajkumar Sharma in an interview many years later. "He was determined, dedicated and wanted to dominate from the first day. He had a tremendous self-belief that he could do anything."

Virat had only been at the academy for a week or two when he gave an early sign of his potential. He was picked with a group of others from the WDCA to play a casual game for under-14 players against another Delhi cricket academy called Playmakers. The match was held at Springdales School, a short distance east of where the Kohlis lived.

Suresh Batra looked on as Virat went out to bat. This young boy needs a lot of coaching, the assistant coach noted. He didn't move his feet much and he lacked certain cricket shots needed to prosper as a top player. But as a ball was bowled, Virat did something remarkable.

SLAP!

Using expert timing and strong wrists, he turned his bat and simply flicked the delivery up and away over the boundary. Those watching were astonished.

"That's a six!"

"My word, what a shot."

"Wrists of steel, and a great eye, as well."

"For a small boy, that was effortless!"

Assistant coach Suresh Batra was impressed.

A Lot to Learn

As he recalled in a newspaper interview years later:

"This boy casually picked the ball off his legs and sent it soaring over mid-wicket. For someone who was not even ten, it was a tremendous shot to play."

It was all very well having confidence and hitting the occasional amazing shot, but Virat quickly found that he had so much to learn. His casual games of gully cricket were nothing like this. He was now playing against a rock-hard cricket ball that was unforgiving and really hurt if it struck you. What's more, he was up against other talented cricketers, some of whom were bigger and more experienced than him.

After a series of nets and practices with children his own age, Virat was unsatisfied. The other children had trouble getting him out when they bowled to him, just like his brother's friends. So, he approached Coach Rajkumar and asked if he could play with the older kids at the academy. He wanted the challenge.

The coach said no at first, but Virat continued to ask him session after session. Rajkumar was a little irritated by Virat's pestering but also intrigued to see how the talkative young trickster would do against the older boys.

The coach relented and Virat got his chance. He coped well at the start, getting into line and defending fast deliveries or swaying out of their way. Then, one ball rose wickedly off the matting wicket and through Virat's guard. It struck him hard on the chest. Virat crumpled to the ground in pain.

"Owww!"

"Kohli's down!"

"He's hurt."

"That was a fearsome ball."

"Poor defence, more like!"

"Phew, he's getting up."

Virat was helped off the pitch, trying to hide his pain and tears from the other boys. An ugly, purple bruise appeared on his chest where he'd been struck. When Saroj Kohli spotted this she insisted Virat returned to playing with boys his own age. But Virat was adamant and told his mum, "I have to play with the older boys so that I can improve." It was one of the few times Virat disagreed with his mother.

Coach Rajkumar knew he had a talent on his hands but was strict and tough with Virat. He had seen too many talented young cricketers fade away through not working hard enough at their game. The coach developed some challenging practices especially for Virat to work on. These were designed to help him with his footwork when batting and to improve his range of strokes.

Virat loved playing flicks and shots off his legs to the on-side of the pitch, also known as the leg side. This sometimes meant that he swung his bat from the off-side across and in front of his legs to the on-side – a method that left him in danger of being out leg before wicket (LBW) if the ball struck his pads.

Coach Rajkumar told him not to play on the on-side so much, but Virat just couldn't help himself. Not when a juicy loose ball just sat there, waiting to be pulled or flicked for runs. So, Rajkumar chose a more extreme option. He banned Virat from playing on-side shots at the academy for several months.

Agony!

However, it forced him to develop his other strokes down the ground and on the off-side. And as they improved, Virat realised that his coach was right all along.

★ CHAPTER 4 ★

At the Academy

Virat spent a lot of his tweens and early teens at the West Delhi Cricket Academy. Chances are if you were visiting there for training drills or a net session between 1999 and 2002, you'd find him there as well, chatting away, practising shots and very rarely being still.

His brother would sometimes take him there. On other occasions, his father ferried him to the ground on the back of his Honda motor scooter, with Virat clinging on for dear life. As Virat entered his teens, he most often cycled the five kilometres himself with his big cricket bag balanced precariously across the handlebars.

According to Coach Rajkumar, Virat was never late for a coaching session and always one of the last cricket students to leave. Sometimes, one of the assistant coaches had to chase him out of the ground to get rid of him!

Virat enjoyed some subjects at school, especially history, but he loathed maths. He already knew that he wanted to become a professional cricketer. At the academy, Virat continued to pester Coach Rajkumar with questions, seeking to learn everything about the sport. When the coach had had enough, he would fold his hands together as a silent signal, commanding Virat to be quiet.

Back at home, Prem and Saroj kept on reminding their young son about the importance of hard work and how he should always follow the advice and instructions of his coaches. Prem was quite a strict father but always supported his sons and daughter. Secretly, both his parents were thrilled at how

At the Academy

Virat was progressing as a cricketer. It was Prem's dream that his son might, one day, play cricket for his country.

Virat may have been restless and talkative, but he was always respectful of his coaches . . . well almost always. Most Sundays at the academy featured a dreaded cross-country run through Delhi's parks and streets. This was far from Virat's favourite part of training. He did not enjoy running five, six or seven kilometres in the Delhi heat. So sometimes, he would get a little help . . .

"Where's Virat? He was lagging behind us ten minutes ago."

"Who cares? Just focus. This run is hard work."

"He's not going to pull that trick again, is he?"

"Do you think so? He has some nerve!"

"Look, there he is, far ahead. He's just getting off a milkman's bike."

"He's missed out half the run. The cheek!"

"Imagine if Coach Rajkumar found out . . ."

It turned out that the coach *did* know.
He often followed the cross-country runners on
his moped without them knowing . . . and he
saw Virat hitch a lift!

When he wasn't ducking out of long runs,
Virat was enjoying his cricket and making
good friends. One of his closest buddies at the
academy was Shalaj Sondhi, a promising spin
bowler. Shalaj's family used to arrive carrying
food for all the young players at games and
practices. Virat was a big fan of Shalaj's mother,
Neha, who he called Auntie. He was an even
bigger fan of her cooking. When she arrived
at the cricket ground with a basket of goodies,
Virat would be the first to shout, "What have
you got there for me, Auntie?"

Cheeky and quick, he was often the first to
fall on the basket of pakoras, samosas and
other tasty treats Mrs Sondhi brought. He'd pull
out the big box of aloo stuffed potatoes – his
favourite. He'd then sprint away around the

edge of the cricket ground, trying to eat as many delicious mouthfuls as possible before the other boys, anxious for a bite, chased and caught him.

When a Sondhi food parcel wasn't available, Shalaj and Virat would often go to street food vendors outside the academy's cricket ground. Training and playing all day saw them work up a big appetite.

Virat really liked going to a Chinese food van called Chuk Chuk Mail. There, he would often tuck into big bowls of manchow soup or chicken fried rice. Sometimes, Shalaj and Virat would turn it into a contest and see how many bowls they could gobble down.

When they weren't eating or playing cricket, Shalaj kept a scrapbook of the academy team. It started filling up with news cuttings of games won and the team's exploits. The scrapbook also contained handwritten profiles of the players in their team. In his profile, Virat listed his favourite colour as black and his most embarrassing moment as, 'Not yet'. When it came to filling in the panel marked 'ambition' Virat wrote, 'To become an Indian cricketer'. Shalaj still has that scrapbook to this day.

Virat, meanwhile, had a long, long way to go to fulfil his dream and play for his country.

CHAPTER 5

Making the Grade

More people watch and play cricket in India than in any other country on Earth. This means that competition for places can be intense – as it was in Delhi junior cricket when Virat was growing up. Dozens of promising players had to sometimes compete for just one or two places in a top team.

You had to be extremely talented to prosper or find another way to get into a team. Some complained that the bigger, richer and more influential clubs got their players selected more than the smaller teams.

The West Delhi Cricket Academy was neither

rich nor influential, but they had produced an exciting young player in 12-year-old Virat Kohli. After scoring heaps of runs for local sides, many cricket watchers thought he was certain to be selected for the Delhi Under-14s team. Coach Rajkumar was one of them.

The evening of the selection announcement was a tense one in the Kohli household. The family waited by the phone all night, but his selection call never came. Virat cried bitter tears that night.

The Kohli family and coaches at the academy had to work hard to rebuild Virat's dented confidence. He bounced back quickly and started scoring heavily again. Not being selected for the Under-14s had lit a fire in him. Playing for less influential sides like the WDCA meant he had to shine even brighter than players at big clubs.

"If someone is getting a hundred, I have to get two hundred. Otherwise, no one is going to notice me," he thought.

The selectors couldn't ignore him for long and in 2002 at the Luhnu Cricket Ground, Virat made his debut for Delhi's Under-15s. Virat only scored 15 from a painstaking 59 balls but in the next match, versus Harayana, his 70 runs settled any nerves. He ended the 2002–03 season as his team's highest run-scorer. Brilliant!

Promoted to captain for the following season, Virat led from the front. Whilst playing against Jammu and Kashmir, he scored 119 – his first century in Zonal cricket. It was a masterpiece of concentration and patience, and took almost six hours of batting as he faced 302 balls. By the end of the season, he was leading run-scorer for Delhi again.

A batter's average is the number of runs they scored divided by the number of times they are out. Virat's average for the 2003–04 season was an incredible 78 runs – more than double his average the previous season.

He was learning to craft long innings, and

it was no surprise when in 2004 he was moved up early to the Delhi Under-17s. In fact, it was a double celebration at the WDCA as he was joined in the squad by his old academy pal, Shalaj, the friend he used to have bets with over who could eat the most food.

The Delhi Under-17s played in the Vijay Merchant Trophy and were coached by Ajit Chaudhary. He liked the look of this new confident batter from the WDCA who was also becoming a great fielder. Coach Chaudhary, though, did not put up with players messing around. On one occasion, he saw Virat lazing around on the cricket ground and not working on his fielding. The coach immediately dropped Virat for the next game. Ouch! Virat was back in the side quickly but had learned the lesson – he needed maximum effort and intensity in training.

Shalaj and Virat got to play together in the Delhi side in December 2004 with telling results. In the game against Himachal Pradesh, Shalaj took four wickets and Virat scored an incredible 251 not out. At one point, Shalaj came out to join Virat at the crease.

"You're playing brilliantly."

"Thanks, Shalaj."

"What should I do?"

"You just have to stand and I will deliver."

Virat was true to his word. He struck 31 fours in his innings and was awarded 11,000 rupees for his man of the match performance. Ten days later, both starred in a great victory over Jammu and Kashmir. Shalaj took 5 for 27 with his spin bowling whilst Virat scored an epic 179, this time striking 33 fours. Matchwinners!

The second season in the Under-17s went even better. Virat was adding power to his shots and learning how to play different bowlers in different conditions. He had mates to rely on in the Delhi side, including Shalaj, and fast bowler Ishant Sharma who he shared the same West Delhi sense of humour with.

Virat scored 227 versus Punjab as Delhi finished top of the North Zone table. He then went one run better, blasting a monstrous 228 in the semi-final of the Vijay Merchant Trophy versus Baroda. Delhi marched on to become champions, with Virat the competition's highest run-scorer notching 757 runs from just nine innings. He'd also shown his skill as a fielder by taking nine catches.

Very well done, Virat!

★ CHAPTER 6 ★

Triumph and Tragedy

Despite his amazing performances, some of the selectors and coaches of the Delhi & District Cricket Association still needed convincing that Virat was the real deal. It took a lot of arguing by Atul Wassan, now the DDCA chairman of selectors, to persuade others that Virat and Ishant Sharma were stellar talents. Some were reluctant to select two untried youngsters from West Delhi.

Atul got his way and both were selected to play in the 2006–07 Ranji Trophy. This is India's nationwide domestic championship, a little like the County Championship in the UK or the

Sheffield Shield in Australia. It was the biggest competition for cricket within India at the time. Understandably, Virat and his family were thrilled. His father had given him a sacred thread as a gift. Virat either wore it around his wrist or kept it carefully in his cricket bag. It meant a lot.

Both Ishant and Virat made their Ranji Trophy debut against Tamil Nadu in November 2006. The Delhi team was led by Mithun Manhas, with the mercurial Shikhar Dhawan as opening bat and Indian left arm Test bowler Ashish Nehra also in the side. Whilst Ishant impressed on debut and took four wickets, Virat struggled and only made ten runs. He did better in his second match reaching 42 before being unluckily run out.

Virat should have been overjoyed at playing Ranji Trophy cricket, but a terrible tragedy had struck the Kohli family. Prem suffered a stroke in November, which left him paralysed down his left side. Virat's dad spent weeks in bed, unable to move much. As Virat reflected later, "He was a self-made man. He was always never dependent on anyone. For a person to go through that was terrible."

His parents made it clear that they wanted their son to continue playing cricket; he had worked so hard to get to this point, they insisted he carry on.

In Virat's next Ranji Trophy match, Delhi were up against Karnataka – a tough team. Boosted by Robin Uthappa hitting 161, Karnataka amassed 446. In reply, Delhi faltered and their fans were dismayed.

"Oh no! Aakash has gone for a duck."

"Clean bowled by Vinny Kumar's fifth ball. We're 0 for 1."

"Now, Mayank has gone. We're 7 for 2."

Back in the dressing room, Virat had his pads on his legs and was ready to bat early. Things were not looking good.

"At least we have the skipper and Shikhar at

the crease," whispered one fan.

The captain, Mithun Manhas, struck a solid four. Perhaps the pressure would ease and Delhi could build a good score.

Not a chance. Within moments, Vinny Kumar struck again and Mithun was out.

"14 for 3. We're in *real* trouble."

Virat strode out across the green turf of the Feroz Shah Kotla Stadium, Delhi's home ground. He was the fifth Delhi batter in and it was only the sixth over. He focused hard and defended the last three balls of the over successfully, but in the next, Shikhar Dhawan was out. Delhi were 14 for 4 and there were another 40 overs that day. Virat set himself a target to still be batting at the end of the day, and began playing patiently. Biding his time, he didn't score off the first 14 balls he faced, but the 15th he struck crisply to the boundary.

At the end of the day, Delhi were 103–5 with Virat still there unbeaten on 40. It had been a gritty display, but Virat knew he and his partner, Punit Bisht, were the last recognised batters in the Delhi side. His team needed a big effort the next day if they were to save the game.

That night, back at home, tragedy struck. Prem Kohli had a heart attack at around 2.30am. The family tried to revive him and raced around their neighbourhood seeking out a doctor. When one couldn't be found, they rushed to hospital, but Virat's father had gone. He died on 18 December 2006, at the age of 54.

His family broke down at the hospital at the news, but Virat couldn't cry. As he later said, "I had no emotion. I was blank. I could not register what happened."

The tears started coming later that early morning when he called his old West Delhi coach, Rajkumar Sharma, to tell him the news. Virat didn't know what to do, but his coach urged him to "show his character" and do what he thought was right.

Amazing Cricket Stars – Virat Kohli

The third day of the match was scheduled to start at 9.30 in the morning. As captain of the team, Mithun Manhas prided himself on getting to the ground nice and early, usually before the rest of the team. Arriving two hours before play began, Mithun was startled to discover his young batter already in the dressing room, head in his hands.

Despite the terrible news, Virat wanted to bat and help his team. He broke down several times as Ishant and the rest of the team arrived and consoled him. His captain ordered him to return home, but Virat refused, saying he and his family thought he should continue to bat as the team needed him. Some of the older players marvelled at the strength of will of their 18-year-old batter.

In a CNN interview in 2016, Virat explained, "I said I wanted to play, because for me not completing a cricket game is a sin. That was a moment that changed me as a person."

Virat lasted almost all of the long morning's

play. By the time he was out, he had scored 90 and Delhi had passed 200. Just as importantly, he had faced 40 overs of bowling, reducing the time left in the game. This helped Delhi obtain the draw they were after. Only then did he return home to help with the preparations and rituals surrounding his father's funeral.

Like many young people who tragically lose a parent, Virat grew up quickly. He was deadly serious about cricket and about honouring his father's memory by playing for his country. Nothing less than total focus and commitment would now do.

★ **CHAPTER 7** ★

A Taste of Glory

Virat stepped off a plane at Kuala Lumpur
International Airport. The air felt muggy and
the sky bright, so he slipped his sunglasses on.
It was February 2008 and the reason for the trip
was HUGE. He was taking part in a World Cup
for the first time.

It had only been 14 months since his father
had died and a lot had happened since.
Every day he thought about his dad as he
continued to forge his career in cricket. He
had been selected for the India Under-19
team, scoring centuries against New Zealand,
Bangladesh and Sri Lanka in 2007. When not

touring with the Under-19s, Virat continued playing for Delhi in Ranji Trophy matches, making centuries against Karnataka and Rajasthan. It was with Delhi that he earned himself a new nickname.

Like many teenagers, Virat was caring more and more about his appearance. After fearing he was losing his hair, he decided to get a close-cropped haircut. Virat returned to hoots of laughter in the Delhi team's dressing room. With his mop of hair gone, his ears and cheeks looked a lot larger, and Coach Chaudhary thought he looked like the cartoon rabbit Chikoo (also known as Chiku) from the comic, *Champak*! Despite Virat's protests, the name stuck and was not only used by his Delhi teammates but later by the Indian national team. Indian captain Mahendra Singh Dhoni was often the worst offender.

'Chikoo' Kohli was in Malaysia with India's Under-19 team not just as a player but as captain. The team he skippered contained plenty of excellent cricketers, including his vice-captain, Ravindra Jadeja, who had appeared at the previous U-19 World Cup in 2006, and fast bowler Siddarth Kaul. The side also contained the opening batter and spinner, Napoleon Einstein.

Virat was mindful that many of the 15 opposing teams at the tournament were also packed with talent. England, for example, boasted Chris Woakes, Liam Dawson and Steven Finn, and Australia's team included Marcus Stoinis, Steve Smith and Josh Hazlewood.

In short videos filmed for the tournament, each player had to name their role in their team and their favourite player. Virat named Herschelle Gibbs of South Africa as his fave player and that he was a "Right-handed batter and a right arm quick bowler." Teammates and Indian cricket commentators were surprised. Virat really wasn't known for his bowling.

But he had a few surprises in store.

In India's first Group B game, versus Papua New Guinea, Virat brought himself on and clean bowled both Joel Tom and Willie Gavera to end with amazing figures of 1.5 overs bowled, two wickets for just four runs.

Then, in their third group game, this time against the West Indies, Virat hit his first tournament century. It was a beautiful and belligerent innings and took just 74 balls. India won by 50 runs and Virat received his first World Cup player of the match award.

India thrashed England, scoring the runs needed with 11 overs to spare. Kohli and Co. were into the Super Semis! Up against them was a star-studded New Zealand squad. It included ace batter Kane Williamson (who would go on to score over 8,000 Test and 6,500 ODI runs) and two fast bowlers, Tim Southee and Trent Boult, who would go on to take 700 Test wickets between them.

New Zealand batted first and Virat caused

a surprise by picking himself to bowl seven of the 50 overs. His first three were pretty uneventful but the game suddenly got more interesting for Indian fans in the fourth.

"In comes Kohli, wider of the crease than usual. Williamson facing, looking balanced and composed on 37. Kohli bowls. It's wide, down the leg side, and Williamson swings but misses and steps out of his crease. It's going upstairs to the TV umpire . . ."

A tense wait followed.

"The replay shows Williamson out of his crease as wicketkeeper Goswami removes the bails with the ball in his right hand. The New Zealand captain is OUT. Stumped! New Zealand are 86 for 3."

Four balls later, Virat was at it again. A ball bowled just outside off stump was missed by the batter, Fraser Colson. The ball angled inwards to nudge the off stump and knock the bail off. OUT! Suddenly, New Zealand were 91 for 4 and in trouble. They did well to score 205.

In reply, Virat came in to bat with his team at 40 for 2. By the time he was out for 43, they had reached 150 with plenty of overs remaining. India won and Virat was player of the match for a second time. Their opponents in the final would be South Africa – Virat was excited. He phoned his old West Delhi Cricket Academy coach. He had one question. Could Rajkumar fly out to Malaysia to watch the final live? The answer was a resounding yes!

Virat had lost all but one of the coin tosses at the tournament prior to the final. He lost again and Wayne Parnell put India into bat. No one in the Indian side really got going. Virat only scored 19, two teammates reached 20 and only Tanmay Srivastava stuck around with 46 precious runs. India's total of 159 was modest and their fans at the Kinrara Academy Oval or watching on TV back in India were down – it looked like India had choked in the final.

A Taste of Glory

Virat gathered his team into a huddle and spoke.

"This could be the match of your life. Forget everything, just give it your best shot. Whatever happens, just don't regret that you didn't give it all you've got."

The team responded to their skipper's stirring words. In next-to-no time, South Africa were 6 for 2, then 11 for 3, then 22 for 4. They were reeling; only Reeza Hendricks and Wayne Parnell provided any resistance. South Africa tumbled to 97 for 6 before Siddarth Kaul took two wickets in the final over. India had won!

As Kaul's final delivery knocked the stump out of the ground, Virat raced to the wicket in joy. He grabbed a stump with one hand as a precious souvenir and fist pumped the air with his other. The rest of the team went nuts. Other players and staff raced onto the field, some carrying Indian flags.

A special plane was chartered to fly the

winning team back home. They arrived jubilant in Bengaluru to a heroes' welcome. Virat and his teammates were honoured in a lavish ceremony at the M. Chinnaswamy Stadium, but were also stunned to find themselves riding on an open-topped bus round the streets of the city, cheered on by big crowds of fans.

"Look at all those people, Virat."

"It's amazing."

"This is crazy!"

"My arms are tired from waving at everyone!"

The Indian cricket board later announced a prize award of 15 lakh (1.5 million) rupees (about £21,000) for each member of the team. The money was nice and welcome, but what struck Virat more was the pride in his team's achievement. "It was the best thing to have happened in my life," he reflected. Millions of Indian cricket fans had tuned in to the tournament on TV especially as India had progressed to the final. They now all knew the name Virat Kohli. His first world cup tournament had provided him with an early taste of success, fame and glory . . . and he liked it!

★ CHAPTER 8 ★

The Number 18

Everything was happening for Virat now. Within months of returning to India, he was selected for the very first Indian Premier League (IPL) season by Royal Challengers Bangalore and had his own business manager. Bunty Sajdeh was a talent scout and manager who had just set up his own business, Cornerstone. He had spotted Virat in action during the Under-19 World Cup when he had been impressed with his confidence and how he spoke. "He has that bit of personality we can work with," Bunty thought.

Most importantly, in those dizzying few months, Virat also got the chance to pull on a full Indian team shirt for the first time. It was emblazoned with the number 18 on its back.

Virat and the number 18 are now linked in many cricket fans' minds. But he didn't pick his playing number like Joe Root chose 66 or Shane Warne chose 23. He actually had no say in the matter. When he was first selected for the Under-19s, he was handed a bag of national team kit for him to wear – an exciting moment for any up-and-coming cricketer. When he examined the clothing, the number 18 was already ironed onto the shirts.

Virat was 18 years old at the time, and later his father sadly died on the 18 December, so the number grew to have great meaning to him. A happier connection occurred on 18 August 2008, when he got the chance to play his first one day international for India. It was a proud moment for Saroj, Vikas, Bhawna and the rest of the Kohli family.

Virat has stuck with 18 but other players have

changed their jersey number. Rahul Dravid, for example, switched from 5 to 19 to remind him of his wife Vijeta's birthday (19 November). Hard-hitting opening batter Virender Sehwag once wore 44, then changed to 46 on the advice of an astrologer. Later, he decided that astrology and lucky numbers didn't help him score runs and for a time played with no number on his back at all!

A stroke of bad luck befell Virender Sehwag whilst in Sri Lanka with India's 2008 one day squad. He twisted his ankle in training, was ruled out, and Virat was given his debut. He was nervous about the game, but more so about meeting his absolute idol, Sachin Tendulkar.

Virat fretted about Sachin for several days beforehand. Cottoning on, some of his new teammates – Yuvraj Singh, Munaf Patel, Irfan Pathan and Harbhajan Singh – convinced him that every debutant performed a ritual the first time they met Tendulkar.

Virat was in the dressing room opposite Sachin. He watched The Little Master lay out his kit methodically. Now was the time.

Virat walked over, dropped to his knees and started to bow his head towards Sachin's feet.

"What are you doing?" gasped Sachin, surprised.

"They told me I had to touch your feet out of respect," replied Virat.

"No, no, no. Such things don't happen," Sachin replied.

Virat got to his feet, feeling his cheeks redden with embarrassment.

"They are just pulling your leg," Sachin added.

Virat looked over at Irfan, Munaf and Yuvraj. They were creased up with laughter.

"Got you Kohli!"

"You should see your face."

PRANKED!

Virat's debut game for India was not what he

had hoped for. He opened the batting with Gautam Gambhir who was out second ball and only lasted 22 balls himself, making 12 runs before being LBW to Nuwan Kulasekara. He scored 37, 25 and 54 in his next three games, and after the Sri Lankan series didn't play for India again for 13 months.

Part of the reason was simple bad luck and the recovery from injury of players like Virender Sehwag. But rumours of Virat's own behaviour were also partly to blame. For the first time in his life, he had spare money in his pocket with contracts with the BCCI (who runs Indian cricket), the IPL and bat sponsorship with Nike. It was exciting and he couldn't resist a few cool clothes, some tattoos and his first car.

It wasn't a sleek sports car, but a chunky Tata Safari SUV. He liked driving a big sports utility vehicle as people tended to get out of its way! But Virat didn't know much about his new car and made an expensive mistake. He and his brother filled the car's fuel tank up with petrol instead of diesel. The car wouldn't run and Virat had a big bill for the tank to be emptied and cleaned. Oops!

Virat enjoyed being in the limelight and was invited to lots of events and parties. The selectors heard exaggerated rumours of his partying, and were concerned. The young man had not scored that heavily in the Sri Lankan series and they worried that his focus wasn't 100 per cent on his cricket. Virat was stunned to be dropped for the next big ODI series, versus New Zealand, and then the next, in 2009, against the West Indies.

Virat sought the advice of those close to him, especially his brother and his old coach, Rajkumar Sharma. In a 2013 interview in *The Hindu* newspaper, Virat called Rajkumar "my guide, mentor, father figure. I'm blessed to have such a wonderful coach. I will always remain grateful to him."

Rajkumar urged Virat to put the disappointment behind him, and just like when he wasn't selected for Delhi Under-14s, use it as fuel to score lots of runs for his other teams. Virat responded with centuries for Delhi in the Ranji Trophy and for the Emerging Players team of Indian cricketers playing in Australia. At the tournament, Virat scored two centuries and 398 runs in total, more than anyone else.

He also focused far less on partying and far more on getting fitter and stronger. He started hitting the gym where he worked with a fitness coach called Basu Shanker. They did all sorts of exercises but especially squats with weights to build up the strength in his legs.

"Come on, one more set. Push, PUSH!"

"Aaargghh!"

"Well done. Now, one more set, Virat."

"Being fitter made me mentally stronger," noted Virat later. "It was a direct connection."

With his strength and fitness improving, the

runs coming in domestic cricket and a better mindset, Virat was hopeful of a return to India's ODI team. And with it, finally, the chance to play with India's greatest ever cricketer.

★ CHAPTER 9 ★

Chak De! India

Although Virat had shared a dressing room with the great Sachin Tendulkar and been pranked by teammates into getting on his hands and knees in front of him, he hadn't yet been picked in the same team as his idol. He couldn't wait for the chance.

Sachin Ramesh Tendulkar was only 16 years old when he first played for India in Tests and ODIs. His poise, balance and timing wowed everyone who saw him in action. Tendu, The Little Master or The Master Blaster (he had a lot of nicknames during his long career), went on to smash many cricketing records. He ended up scoring more Test (15,921) and ODI (18,426) runs than any other player ever! He also notched more Test centuries (51) and more one day centuries (49) than anyone else, and in 1998 scored an incredible 1,894 runs in ODIs alone.

Virat was in awe of Sachin's talent, but close up to him in the same squad, he was even more impressed by his dedication and perfectionism. Sachin was always disciplined and focused. Virat vowed he must be the same. "I learnt humility from him, I learnt absolute commitment to the sport," Virat said of Tendulkar.

In turn, Sachin saw that Virat was passionate and dedicated. "He had the fire in him, I could see that hunger," he recalled.

Virat was called up after injuries to Sehwag and Gambhir for India's tilt at the 2009 Compaq Cup ODI competition. Virat was selected for the final along with Sachin and his old West Delhi pal, Ishant Sharma. Their opponents were the hosts, Sri Lanka.

Virat expected to bat at the start of India's innings, but in the end was sent in at number 7. He could only watch on in amazement at the R. Premadasa Stadium in Colombo as, in the sticky heat, Sachin put on a batting masterclass. Rasping drives, delicate glances, sweeps and reverse sweeps, The Little Master played them all as he scored 138 runs. By the time Virat got to bat, Sachin had gone, and he only got to face two balls.

India won, but Virat knew that unless he seized the next chance given to him, he was in danger of being thought of as a handy substitute batter and not a first-choice pick. The chance came in the ICC Champions Trophy a mere month later. After getting out for just 16 in his first game, Virat lay awake all night, replaying his bad shot over and over again and fearing for his place in the side.

Four days later, he strode out to bat with India 12 for 2 in the fourth over. This might be his last chance to impress, and the West Indian pace bowler, Kemar Roach, was racing in hard and bowling extremely FAST.

Kemar's first ball to Virat was measured at 153 kilometres per hour – that's really, really rapid. It struck Virat's bicep but he refused to show any pain. Inside, though, he was thinking, "One hundred and fifty-three clicks . . . how the hell am I gonna ever score runs at this level?"

Virat defended the next two balls, then, as Kemar bowled a little wider, he unfurled a booming square cut to smash the ball to the boundary. That felt better, and some of the tension drained out of him.

Twenty-eight overs later, Virat stepped out of his crease to hit a straight drive shot. He mistimed it a little but it sped past a fielder and Virat and his batting partner, Abhishek Nayar, were able to trot through for a single. It was the game's winning run. Virat was 79 not out and won the player of the match.

"If I can do this more often, surely I can go on for a long time," he thought.

Virat scored his first ODI century for India just five matches later at India's biggest cricket stadium, Eden Gardens. He and Gautam Gambhir both scored hundreds, and Gambhir was awarded player of the match. But just as he was to receive the trophy, a new smartphone and a giant cheque, Gautam handed all the prizes to Virat. "The way Kohli batted took a lot of pressure off my shoulders," he told reporters. Virat was thrilled to have made a hundred for India and impressed a more experienced teammate.

Virat made three more centuries before the 2011 ICC World Cup began. For India, who were joint hosts along with Sri Lanka and Bangladesh, this tournament was a BIG deal. It gripped the nation. The title song from an Indian sports film *Chak De! India* (Go! India) became an unofficial slogan of the tournament. Packed crowds would often sing the song to urge their heroes on. Games were noisy and atmospheric.

It helped that India got off to a winning start, and for that they could thank Virender Sehwag and their youngest batter, 22-year-old Virat Kohli. Both scored centuries to take India to a total of 370. Virat's hundred took just 83 balls as he blazed eight fours and two towering sixes. He was the only Indian player to ever score a century in his first ICC World Cup match.

India's batting prowess saw them march through the tournament to the final against Sri Lanka in the Wankhede Stadium in Mumbai. Some 40,000 spectators crammed in – the place was a riot of noise and colour. Hundreds of millions of Indian fans tuned in at home, willing their side on. India hadn't won this competition since 1983, before Virat was born. They knew that it would be Sachin Tendulkar's last one day game for his country. He was retiring afterwards.

Sri Lanka scored 274 for 6 – a challenging

total. Their number one fast bowler was Lasith Malinga. His unusual bowling action with a very low arm helped the ball move away from the edge of right-handers' bats. He was bowling well and had already dismissed Virendar Sehwag with the second ball of the innings. Now he thundered in to bowl the first ball of a new over at Sachin Tendulkar on his home ground. Fans in the stadium watched on tensely.

"Nooooo! He's edged it!"

"Kumar's caught him." Kumar Sangakkara was Sri Lanka's brilliant wicketkeeper and batter.

"Tendu's out. 31–2. Who's in next?"

"Virat Kohli."

"The kid? I hope he plays well."

Virat's chance of batting with The Little Master in the final had been squashed. The pair passed each other on the ground, Virat jogging out to bat, Sachin retreating to the dressing room. They shared just a handful of words as they crossed. They were easy to hear as the ground had gone spookily silent . . . apart from small pockets of Sri Lankans cheering wildly.

"Careful. The ball is still swinging," said Sachin.

"I understand, Tendu," replied Virat.

"Build a partnership, Virat."

Malinga was really fired up now and Virat had the rest of his over to face. The first ball was a snorter, pitching short and rearing up at his head. Virat ducked out of its way. Phew! That was fast.

Virat focused and reminded himself of what Sachin had said. He defended the rest of the over from Malinga then began building an 83-run partnership with Gautam Gambhir. It could have been more, but Virat was out to a spectacular and unlikely catch. He was furious with himself, but he had helped India take a big step towards their target and later admitted, "It was probably the most valuable 35 runs of my career."

When India's captain MS Dhoni struck

a massive six to win the game, Virat and the rest of the Indian team charged onto the pitch. Fireworks went off above the stadium, thumping drums erupted in the crowd. It was chaos!

"Yes, Yes, YESSSSS!"

"*Chak De!* India."

"Champions!"

Virat hugged all his teammates. Some were on the ground waving Indian flags. Others were crying. Harbhajan Singh was doing both!

As the team started a victory lap around the ground, Virat hoisted Sachin onto his shoulders. He carried him around the outfield. The noise from the fans was deafening. Virat understood that for Sachin to win such a big prize near the end of his career was amazing, especially as Mumbai was Sachin's home city.

A microphone was poked in front of Virat during the celebrations. He was jubilant and shouted, "This goes out to all the people of India. This is my first World Cup, I can't ask for more. Tendulkar has carried the burden of the nation for 21 years. It was time we carried him. *Chak De!* India!"

★ CHAPTER 10 ★

Attacking the Aussies

Three months later, Virat was not only a World Cup winner but a Test match player when he got his chance in a three-match series in the West Indies.

Test cricket is the peak of the sport. Matches are played for up to five days in a row with each team getting two innings to bat. Each match pushes batters, bowlers and fielders to the limit – that's why it's called a Test with a capital T! Virat called it "the most beautiful format of the game," and added "nothing comes close to playing an intense game in whites – what a blessing to be able to play Test cricket for India."

Virat's Test debut came in Jamaica on 20 June 2011. It was much like his ODI debut: a bit disappointing. It started well, with his first Test runs coming from a four tickled down the leg side off pacy fast bowler Fidel Edwards. Fidel quickly obtained revenge, though. Virat was out cheaply to him in both innings, scoring just 19 runs in the match. His next three Test innings were 0, 27 and 30. Virat was already under pressure for his place.

In an interview with Sriram Veera on *ESPN Cricinfo*, Virat sounded calm. "It's just a matter of things going my way. I know I am batting well . . . One innings can turn things around for you . . . I'm working really hard for that."

It helped having Sachin around. He hadn't been part of the India team in the Caribbean but he did return by the time Virat played his fourth Test match of 2011. The opponents were the West Indies again, but this time back in India. Sachin scored 94 in the first innings whilst

Attacking the Aussies

Virat scored 52 in the first and 63 in the second innings.

Virat got to spend more cricketing time with Sachin before The Little Master retired, absorbing every bit of advice he could. The pair finally got the chance to produce some big batting partnerships. At the 2012 Asia Cup, for example, Virat was at the other end of the pitch as Sachin scored a sparkling 114 versus Bangladesh. In the next game, it was Sachin's turn to marvel, as Virat thrashed a ferocious innings of 183 to defeat India's fiercest rival, Pakistan.

Sachin finally retired from all cricket in 2013. His last match was at the Wankhede stadium in Mumbai. After the game, Virat gifted a tearful Sachin the sacred thread given to him by his late father, Prem Kohli.

"This is the most valuable thing I have," Virat said. "I just want you to know how much you've inspired me and what you mean to all of us. This is my little gift to you."

Sachin was deeply touched by the kind gesture and kept the thread safely. But some time later, he returned it to Virat, saying, "This is priceless. This has to stay with you and no one else."

It wasn't only Tendulkar who Virat absorbed advice from. He still called his old coach, Rajkumar Sharma, between series and listened intently to batting veteran VVS Laxman who'd scored four centuries in Australia. Virat's fifth to eighth Test matches were held in that country, a place where India had never won a series.

VVS explained how Australian pitches were harder and faster than in India. As a result, the ball whizzed through and you had very little time to pick your shot. The fans could also be as hostile as the bowling. It all made playing games in Australia very challenging . . . as Virat soon found out.

"Howzat?"

"It's gotta be LBW."

"He's out, LBW to Ben Hilfenhaus!"

Attacking the Aussies

"Kohli's gone for a golden duck."

"Quack! Quack!"

"Ha, ha, see ya later, loser."

"What a mug!"

Virat trudged back to the pavilion without scoring after facing just one ball in the first Test. Ben Hilfenhaus had got him out in the first innings as well, for just 11 runs. India slumped to a dismal defeat.

The second Test didn't go much better. As Australia were piling on the runs, he was fielding close to the Australian fans in the Sydney Cricket Ground and was receiving a lot of verbal abuse. He put up with it until terrible things were said about his mother and sister. He lost his cool and made a rude gesture to the crowd. He was fined half his entire match fee as a result.

India and Australia moved on to Perth and the WACA ground – home to one of the hardest, fastest and nastiest wickets in world cricket. Virat put the troubles at Sydney behind him to top-score for India in both innings. His knocks of 44 and 75 impressed cricket fans and teammates. Indian spinner Harbhajan Singh noted, "Virat became an even more dangerous player on wickets that were difficult to bat on."

The fourth and final Test was held at the Adelaide Oval, and again India found themselves in trouble. Australia had built up a huge score of 604 and in reply, India had lost Sehwag, Gambhir, Tendulkar and Dravid for less than 90 runs before Virat came to the crease. Not long after, VVS Laxman was also out – India were well and truly on the ropes.

Virat was patient and disciplined. The Australian bowlers were well on top and he had to defend well. He only hit one four in the first 71 balls he faced, but it was a beautiful shot.

"What a stroke that is. Boy, he times the ball nicely, this guy," exclaimed TV commentator Mark Nicholas.

Virat gradually got on top of the bowling. There were lots of scampered ones and twos before he reached his fifty with a lovely drive along the ground. Even some of the opposing fans in the stands were impressed.

"Aw, that's one heck of a shot."

"This kid is coming good."

"We need to get him out."

Into the sixties and Virat launched a ball from Michael Clarke into the stands. SIX!

"He hit that as clean as a whistle," said ex-Australian captain Mark Taylor on commentary.

Wickets were tumbling, though. Three fell when Virat was stranded on 91. At least it brought a familiar face out to be his latest batting partner – his old friend from West Delhi, Ishant Sharma.

Virat's time in the 'nervous nineties' nearly saw him lose his wicket. Twice he played and missed at balls and then on 99, nearly got run out. When he did finally stroke the ball into the covers to run through for his hundred, he was so pumped up that he celebrated violently and nearly forgot to take a second run.

Virat Kohli from the West Delhi Cricket Academy was now a Test match centurion.

"Superb," purred commentator Tony Gregg, "from a guy who's desperately trying to make a difference in this Indian side."

When Virat was finally out for 116, the crowd at the Adelaide Oval rose to applaud the young Indian off the field. In the space of a couple of Test matches, he had won over many Australian cricket fans with his brilliance.

Virat bagged two more Test centuries in 2012 (both scores of 103) then a 107 versus Australia in early 2013 to win in Chennai, India. He was now starting to feel he belonged at this level. "I cannot explain to you the job satisfaction that you get when you do well in Test cricket," Virat stated in an interview, "because you know how demanding it is."

Attacking the Aussies

By the time he returned to Australia in 2014, he was unstoppable! Despite being smashed on the helmet by a Mitchell Johnson bouncer in the very first ball he faced in the series, Virat played brilliantly. He racked up two big centuries of 169 and 147 later in the series but in that first match, held at the Adelaide Oval, he scored hundreds in both innings.

In total, Virat has scored over 2,000 Test runs against Australia and more than 2,200 runs in ODIs, but he remembers his first two Tests at Adelaide particularly fondly . . . especially as in the 2014 match, he led India out onto the pitch for the first time.

★ CHAPTER 11 ★

Captain Fantastic

5 September in India is Teachers' Day. It's a day when former students thank and celebrate their teachers and tutors. On Teachers' Day 2014, Coach Rajkumar Sharma opened his door to find Virat's brother, Vikas, standing there. Vikas handed Rajkumar his phone. On the other end was Virat, away in America.

"Happy Teachers' Day, sir," Virat said.

Vikas placed something in the coach's hand. It was a set of car keys. Virat had bought Rajkumar a brand-new car. Awesome!

Virat often mentioned how his coach had taught him much about cricket, leadership and life. He would need to use all those lessons learned three months later when a statement was announced by the BCCI – the organisation that runs cricket in India.

Virat Kohli will lead India in the first Test.

It took a while to sink in. Virat couldn't quite believe he would be captaining his country's Test team against the mighty Aussies. MS Dhoni had been captain for almost 60 matches since 2008, but he was out of the side for the moment because of a thumb injury.

It was the proudest possible day when Virat led the team out onto the neatly trimmed grass of the Adelaide Oval in December 2014. Sadly, India were outplayed by Australia for much of the first Test but Virat's aggressive tactics gave his side an outside chance of victory on the final day.

Instead of batting slowly for a draw, the team set off on a run chase, needing 364. Virat was in sparkling form and found gritty support from the opening batter Murali Vijay at the other end. The pair took the score to 242–2 and it looked like an epic victory was on. But then Murali was out for 99 and other wickets tumbled. Virat reached 141 before he was out to Nathan Lyon. In the end, India fell short by 48 runs in a gripping game, but Virat's leadership was praised as fresh and exciting.

MS Dhoni returned to lead India in the second Test but minutes after the third Test had finished in a draw he shocked his teammates. MS retired from Test cricket. All eyes were suddenly on Virat. He would be the new permanent captain.

He returned to his room thinking about what it all meant. Memories of all the hundreds of games he had played, the setbacks and triumphs he'd experienced, all came flooding back. It was all too much, and he broke down in tears. Later, he phoned his family and Coach Rajkumar to share the news.

Virat had a good idea of how he wanted India to play. In the past, India had sometimes been too timid and happy to accept a draw when they could be bolder and go for a win. He wanted his side to be brave, full of self-belief and stick together. In a 2015 interview in *The Cricket Monthly*, he said, "I want to create strong bonds. I want to create strong friendships in this unit. We live 250–280 days a year together . . . so, you want to be the team which enjoys each other's company, which enjoys success together and sticks around in failures together."

Some wondered whether being captain would affect his batting. They needn't have worried. Virat scored a century in each of his first three innings as skipper. No one had ever done that before in Test matches. But could he change the way India play, and would it be successful?

It didn't look likely on his first full overseas tour as captain, as India went 1–0 down to Sri Lanka. But the team roared back and won the series

2–1, then thrashed South Africa 3–0. This was the start of an incredible run for Virat's side. They defeated New Zealand three Tests to none, then mauled England 4–0. India were on fire! They went unbeaten in 19 Tests in a row from 2015 to 2017 – quite some achievement.

Fifteen of those 19 unbeaten Tests were wins rather than draws – proof of Virat's attacking tactics. He preferred aggressive bowlers and batters and dropped veteran wicketkeeper Wriddhiman Saha for the explosive batting of 20-year-old Rishabh Pant, even though the youngster was still a newbie to wicketkeeping and made mistakes.

In 2017, Virat replaced MS Dhoni as skipper of India's ODI team. He also often captained the T20i team as well. What a responsibility!

Virat was trying to change how India's national teams acted and played. He was modelling the side on himself – confident and fearless. He pushed the players to train harder to become faster, fitter and better fielders. You didn't want to catch Captain Kohli's steely glare when you messed up a catching drill or looked lazy and sloppy when fielding. Not that Virat was always stern; he could make his teammates laugh with some silly dancing, a lame joke or impressions of famous Indian celebrities. But he also knew when the team needed to ramp it up, get more intense and go for victory.

In the 2021 Test at Lord's, for example, Virat's team had set England 272 to win. It wasn't a big target and he sensed his players appeared too relaxed as they went out to field. This was not what he was after. He wanted a tense atmosphere and pressure put on the England batters.

So, he gathered his team into a huddle. The chatter stopped as Virat spoke.

"If I see anyone laughing in front of their players, see what happens. Got it?"

The players nodded.

"For 60 overs they (the England batters) should feel like hell out there. Attack!"

"Okay, Captain."

Within two overs, England had lost two wickets. After 22 overs, they were 67 for 5. India's bowlers, Jasprit Bumrah, Ishant Sharma and Mohammed Siraj, were on fire. Just as Virat had asked for, India raised their intensity and England crumbled to 120 all out. India won the match and later the series 2–1. In total, India won 40 and drew 11 of 68 Tests that Virat led them into as captain – a brilliant record. As ODI captain, he also won 65 matches (plus three ties) out of 95 games.

But Virat the successful captain was eclipsed by Virat the run machine when he started making big, big scores in 2016 onwards . . .

CHAPTER 12

Best Batter on the Planet

21 July 2016. Virat struck his first Test double hundred. This 200 against the West Indies – included 96 runs in fours alone – was the start of a rich period of run-scoring form.

Virat had scored 11 centuries in his first 41 Tests but had only passed 150 once. England batter Graham Gooch talked about making Daddy Hundreds, meaning that you didn't settle for 110 or 120 but push on to score 170, 180 or more. Virat was keen to score some big, big centuries, and his first 200 triggered more. In 2017, he became the first player to score four double-hundreds in four consecutive Test series (against West Indies, New Zealand, England and Bangladesh). No one else has managed this feat in more than 2,500 Test matches.

In 2017, Virat struck ten centuries for India in Tests and ODIs, becoming the first captain of any country to score so many hundreds in a single year. Indian fans were raving about King Kohli. So were cricket experts. Former Australian captain Steve Waugh said Virat "has got the best technique of anyone in world cricket"; Joe Root labelled him "the most complete player"; West Indian legend Brian Lara described his batting as "unbelievable", and Dwayne Bravo called Virat "the Cristiano Ronaldo of Cricket".

Meanwhile, poor opposition bowlers were worried and wondering, how did they solve a problem like Virat? How should they bowl to him?

Bowl the ball wide to the off-side?

Virat would lean into a delicious cover drive sending the ball racing away to the boundary.

Bowl at his legs?

Best Batter on the Planet

With sweet timing, he'd clip the ball off his legs for one, two or four runs.

Bowl full?

Virat's defence was watertight. He might play a defensive shot or go on the attack and drive the ball straight down the ground. Four!

Bowl short?

Quick as a flash, Virat would swivel, pull and hook your delivery for four or six.

Whilst bowlers tried to solve the puzzle, Virat helped himself to a lot of runs, scoring 2,595 for India in 2016 and besting that the following year with 2,818. Awesome.

At the start of 2018, India were playing in South Africa. Virat scored yet another Test century (his 21st) but had a medical problem. He was in pain, wasn't sleeping and couldn't feel his little finger at all – not good when you're one of the world's leading batters. It turned out that he had a problem with his spine that was pressing on a nerve leading to his little finger.

This was caused by his body taking calcium from his bones, making them a little weaker.

To help his recovery, Virat made some lifestyle changes. He had altered his diet before, cutting out fast food and fried dishes like parathas in favour of healthier options. "I felt a second or two quicker, I was able to react to the ball quicker and my game absolutely changed from there on," he said of his improving diet in 2017. The only problem was that it upset his mum. "I get scolded by my mother. She thinks I am too thin," he said. "She will understand the difference later, I am sure."

Now he made another change, giving up all meat, including favourite dishes like butter chicken. Veggie Virat told Kevin Pietersen in a 2020 video interview, "I've never felt better in my life, to be honest. I've never felt better waking up or recovering after a game."

The change in diet served Virat well in all forms of cricket. He scored 2,735 runs for India in 2018. These included 1,202 one-day runs at an incredible average of 133.6 each time he batted. By October of that year, Virat had become the fastest to score 10,000 runs in ODIs, beating Sachin Tendulkar's record by 54 innings. He ended 2018 ranked as the world number one Test batter and won both the ICC World Test and World ODI Cricketer of the Year awards.

Many people would be satisfied with a stellar year like 2018, but Virat wanted more. He thirsted to lead India to further victories abroad. Virat led India into a four-Test series in Australia at the end of 2018. At the press conference before one of these matches, he said, "If you want to win a series away from home, it has to be an obsession."

Virat led from the front, scoring 259 runs whilst Jasprit Bumrah took 20 wickets in the first three Tests. India led Australia 2–1 going into the final Test at the SCG (Sydney Cricket Ground) and posted a formidable total of 622. Australia were 300 all out and had just started their second innings when rain ended the match. India had won the series and how fans watching on TV back in India celebrated.

"King Kohli's the first Indian captain to win a Test series in Australia."

"*Chak de!* India."

"Brilliant!"

"After 72 years of playing Australia, *finally* we win a series there."

Speaking straight after the match, Virat was ecstatic.

"By far, this is my biggest achievement. It's at the top of the pile. This win will give us a different identity as an Indian team and can inspire kids to do the same for the country going forward."

Later that year, Virat passed 20,000 runs in all forms of cricket for India and gained a significant honour in his home city. The pavilion of the Ferez Shah Kotla Stadium (renamed the Arun Jaitley Stadium), where he had played many games for Delhi teams, was renamed after him. Virat is one of just three current cricketers with part of a major ground named after them (Jimmy Anderson and Darren Sammy being the others).

Mind you, the Virat Kohli Pavilion is not the only sign of Virat's fame you will find in India . . .

★ CHAPTER 13 ★

Virushka

When he was still a young boy, Virat had been walking around Delhi with 'Auntie' – Neha Sondhi, the mother of his great friend, Shalaj. He looked up and saw a giant Bollywood movie poster featuring a dashing hero and a glamorous heroine.

"One day, Auntie," Virat said, "I'll become a very big person and I'll marry a heroine."

Auntie smiled, but Virat was right!

By the time he was in his mid-twenties, Virat Kohli was a 'very big person'. In a cricket-mad country containing more than 1.4 billion people (more than 20 times larger than the UK), the captain of the national cricket team is always one of India's most famous celebrities.

Virat's intensity and run-scoring feats on the pitch, and his confidence and clear speaking off the pitch, made him especially popular with young people. There is even an animated cartoon series called *Super V* loosely based on his life which is shown on TV. If you visit India, you will also see his face on many advertising billboards, in magazines and TV commercials.

In 2013, Virat's manager, Bunty Sajdeh, arranged for the cricketer to appear in one of his first TV adverts, for a shampoo. He was to act and dance alongside celebrated Bollywood actress Anushka Sharma. She had appeared in films including *Rab Ne Bana Di Jodi* and the 2010 smash hit rom-com, *Band Baaja Baaraat*.

Virat fretted about meeting Anushka. "She was one of the well-established, top actors already in India. As soon as I heard that, I started shivering. How the hell am I gonna do this ad with her? She was a proper actor. I was so nervous."

He needn't have worried. Virat and Anushka joked around on the film set for three days and got on very well. Virat was bowled over by the actress's personality and the pair became friends. They later started dating but kept their relationship as secret as they could . . . although Virat would sometimes give things away such as blowing her a kiss when scoring a half century in a match.

Eventually, though, the public got to know all about them, and they became one of India's most famous celebrity couples. They even gained their own joint name – *Virushka*. When they got married in Italy in 2017, just a few of their closest friends including Sachin Tendulkar and Coach Rajkumar attended the wedding, but in a reception back in Delhi, India's Prime Minister was one of the guests.

Virat and Anushka live in a luxury 35th-floor

apartment with its own gym. The apartment gives birds-eye views of Mumbai whilst Virat's former teammate, Yuvraj Singh, is a neighbour, six floors down. The couple also own a family home in Delhi and a farmhouse in Alibaug, a town on India's coast.

Virat is well paid as a top cricketer, but extra wealth has come from advertising and sponsorship. Businesses have queued up to secure his services to promote their products. Virat has some 30 brand deals endorsing everything from sportswear to stationery, vitamins to tyres.

One of his deals is with Audi India. Ever since he bought a chunky SUV as his first vehicle, Virat has been a bit of a car nut. "I do like to step out in my car, enjoy myself and listen to good music," Virat says.

He owns a fleet of vehicles including an Audi R8 sports car, Bentley Continental and a Land Rover Vogue. He admits that some of the cars in his garages are "impulse buys", such as a Lamborghini Gallardo supercar, which he has since sold. He's even taken his cars on to racetracks to see just how fast he can go. One session at the Buddh International Circuit saw him push his Audi R8 past 290 kilometres per hour.

Virat owns and co-owns a number of businesses. Some, like his fashion brand One8 and his One8 Commune restaurants, are named after his shirt number. No surprise that as a fitness fanatic he also co-owns a chain of gyms called Chisel, whilst in 2014 he became co-owner of FC Goa, an Indian Super League football club.

Back in 2013, Virat set up a foundation to raise money for charities and schemes that help underprivileged children. The VK Foundation now also donates to health and animal welfare schemes. Virat and Anushka donate their time and money to a wide range of other charities as well.

From a modest upbringing in West Delhi, Virat

has become one of the most recognisable faces in India. In 2018, *Time* magazine went further and listed him as one of the 100 most influential people in the world. "Being a role model for the young people is no doubt a great feeling," Virat told the Indo-Asian News Service. "But it also carries a huge responsibility, as everything I do and say affects a lot of people."

Virat felt that responsibility keenly, especially when his batting form took a dip, starting in 2020.

★ CHAPTER 14 ★

Slump!

India vs England, Fourth Test, 5 March 2021.

Ben Stokes bounded in to bowl.

Virat waited, eyes wide and bat gripped in his hands.

He had survived seven balls so far, but England's big all-rounder was bowling with good pace and the pitch at Ahmedabad was beginning to play tricks.

"Howzat!"

The ball had whistled past, caught the edge of Virat's bat and landed safely in the hands of England's wicketkeeper, Ben Foakes.

Umpire Virender Sharma slowly raised his finger.

"That's OUT!"

Virat stared at the pitch for a second in disbelief then turned and slowly trudged off for nought, his second duck of the series. He returned to the dressing room to watch the rest of the team prosper with a century from Rishabh Pant and 96 for Washington Sundar. Ishant Sharma, his old pal from West Delhi was also out to Stokes for a duck a little later, but he was a fast bowler and batted number ten in the team; he wasn't a record-breaking batter like Virat.

Virat had started to suffer a batting slump. Despite the occasional solid 50, he was getting out early more than usual. Shortly before England had visited India, he'd led the team to New Zealand. His scores in the two-Test series were a measly 2, 19, 3 and 14. There would be two more ducks to come in Tests in 2021 and other low scores in between. What was going on?

Some experts thought the lack of games he had played recently was the problem.

Slump!

India played far fewer matches in 2020 and 2021 than usual due to the COVID pandemic. COVID also caused the cancellation of tours, T20 games and the Ranji Trophy. Virat and Anushka set up a fund to help some of the many Indians devastated by the pandemic, but he only got to play three Test matches in 2020 and three ODIs in 2021.

Virat thought he was batting reasonably well. He had been an international cricketer for a long time now and knew if his game was going well or not. And just a few months earlier he had won an amazing prize – being awarded the ICC Male Cricketer of the Decade.

But as big scores continued to elude him throughout 2021, the newspapers, websites and TV shows were full of cricket experts discussing what may be wrong with King Kohli.

"It's technical faults with his batting."

"I disagree. His technique is fine, it's his concentration."

"I think he's tired. He's been playing every format of cricket for a long time."

"He became a new parent in January. Perhaps sleepless nights are causing issues?"

"And he's not getting younger. Maybe, he's losing his quick reactions."

The arrival of Vamika, Virat and Anushka's daughter in 2021, had brought him nothing but joy and he felt his technique and reactions were fine. Perhaps his workload as captain and batter in all three formats of the game was the problem?

In September 2021, Virat took action. He stepped down as captain of India's T20 team, and as skipper of the Test side in January 2022. In between, the Indian selectors took away his captaincy of the national ODI team. He made it clear to everyone how he wanted to continue playing as a batter. Part of his statement to the press when he gave up the Test captaincy said:

"It's been seven years of hard work, toil and relentless perseverance every day to take the team in the right direction. I've done the job with absolute honesty and left nothing out there."

In 2021, Ben Stokes had taken a big break from cricket to recharge himself. At the time, Virat had applauded the move and admired Ben's courage. Now, his thoughts turned to himself and whether something similar might help. Despite giving up the captaincies, Virat still didn't feel quite right. "I wasn't excited to practise and that really disturbed me because this is not who I am," he explained in a later interview. Something had to change.

In July 2022, Virat took a break from cricket. He didn't pick up a cricket bat for more than a month. Instead, he relaxed and talked with Anushka and his family. Fans were worried. Would he still have the hunger and desire to return? Was this the end of the Kohli era?

Top batters like Babar Azam and Aussie legend Ricky Ponting didn't think so. Speaking on The ICC Review podcast, Ricky called Virat "a champion player" and someone you "can never write off". He expected Virat to dig deep and find a way to score again.

Would Ricky be proven right?

★ **CHAPTER 15** ★

Make Every Day Super

After six weeks away, Virat returned for the 2022 Asia Cup – a T20i competition, feeling refreshed and eager to train, practise and play again. He was determined to make every day he was part of the India team, a super day. But would the runs come?

In India's first match, he was India's joint top-scorer as they beat Pakistan. In the second match, he scored a fluent 59 and in the third, scored 60.

In India's fifth and final Asia Cup game, Virat faced Afghanistan whose bowlers included the world number one ranked Rashid Khan – an amazing spinner and competitor. Virat was up for the challenge. He opened the batting with KL Rahul and launched Rashid for a four, then a six. In a flash, he was waving his bat to the crowd as they applauded his fifty off just 32 balls.

The 13th over was eventful with two singles, two sixes and two Indian wickets. Virat survived and was joined in the middle by Rishabh Pant. Virat then launched another ball from Rashid Khan for six. The crowd at the Dubai International Cricket Stadium were impressed.

"Wow, he charged down the pitch to Khan. Few batters do that."

"He's into the sixties now."

"Do you know, he's never scored a T20i century?"

"Only four overs left – not time to do it today."

But Virat loves nothing more than proving his doubters wrong and he accelerated. His next series of shots went:

Four!

Four!

Two!

Four!

Two!

Four!

A single off the last ball of the 18th over took him to 90. Virat had kept the strike and was now facing fast-medium bowler Fareed Ahmad. Fareed's first ball pitched only to be smashed back down the ground with tremendous force. It crashed into the boundary. Four! Virat had now passed his previous highest score in T20i games.

The next ball was bowled and pitched a little shorter. Quick as a flash, Virat swivelled on one leg and struck a wicked pull shot. Six! As it soared over the deep midwicket boundary, he flashed a wide smile and held up his bat.

"Yes!"

An incredible 1,021 days since he had last scored a century for India, Virat had got there. It had taken him just 53 balls – that is rapid.

Virat looked up to the sky and was embraced in a big hug from his batting partner. He then reached into his shirt, pulled out his wedding ring, which he keeps on a necklace during matches, and kissed it. He scored 122 not out and in a post-innings interview, dedicated his 71st hundred in international cricket to his wife.

"I am standing here because . . . one person stood by me through all this. This hundred is dedicated to Anushka and our little daughter, Vamika, as well."

Social media was awash with congratulations from fans and fellow players wowed by the elegance of some of his shots and super speedy scoring; his last 63 runs had come off just 21 balls!

Virat entered 2023 in good spirits . . . and good form. Either side of Christmas, he scored 113 in an ODI against Bangladesh then another 113, this time in an ODI against Sri Lanka. He followed that up five days later with another century against Sri Lanka, this time a rollicking 166 not out. Virat was rocking!

He scored two centuries and six half-centuries in the 2023 IPL, becoming the first player to score more than 7,000 IPL runs. The drought was over, but Virat still craved a big Test match score. His last had come in November 2019, 23 Tests ago.

Australia were visiting India and in the first and second Tests, Virat failed to score a century – although he did pass 25,000 runs in international cricket. He joined an elite club with only five other members – including Sachin Tendulkar – but Virat achieved the feat in the fewest number of innings: 549 in total.

He saved his best for the fourth and final Test held in Ahmedabad. India were leading the series 2–1, but Australia had made a big total of 480. So, India needed to bat for a long time to protect their series lead. Virat was up for the fight and was patient. During his epic innings that lasted 8 hours and 37 minutes, he faced 364 balls from the Australian attack. Try as they might, Mitchell Starc, Nathan Lyon and the others couldn't get him out.

He celebrated his 28th Test match hundred and his first in 1,205 days by kissing his wedding ring again. India's innings ended on 571 when he was last man out for a whopping 186. The 45,000-strong crowd at the Narendra Modi Stadium went wild!

Virat nearly added to his tally of 78 centuries in all formats during India's first ICC 2023 World Cup match where India were 2 for 3 and in terrible trouble against Australia. He hit a brilliant 85 to grab India an important victory.

It was just the start, as Virat went on a roll and India went unbeaten for ten games in a row. A 55 not out in the next match was followed by a fizzing century against Bangladesh. Virat's 103 not out was reached with a massive six over mid-wicket and saw him win yet another player of the match award. Scores of 95 (v New Zealand), 88 (v Sri Lanka) and 51 (v the Netherlands) were sandwiched by another Virat masterclass on his birthday against South Africa. He celebrated turning 35 with 101 not out, tying the world record 49 ODI centuries of his mentor, Sachin Tendulkar.

Two games later, in the World Cup semi-final against New Zealand, Virat thumped a marvellous 117 in front of a Wankhede Stadium crowd that included Virat's wife, David Beckham and Sachin Tendulkar. Virat had reached 50 ODI hundreds in just 279 innings, 172 less than Tendulkar and was overwhelmed by his achievement as he looked up at the steep banks of fans in the arena.

"My life partner (Anushka), the person I love the most, she is sitting there. My hero Sachin is sitting there. I was able to get the 50th in front of them and all these fans in such an historic venue. It was amazing."

In total, Virat's 2023 World Cup saw him score

three centuries and six half-centuries, the last coming in the final which India lost to Australia. Virat ended the tournament as its leading run scorer with 765 runs at an average of 95.62 and was awarded the Player of the World Cup. Any thoughts of that slump a few years earlier had been well and truly forgotten.

Four years before his epic performances at the 2023 World Cup, Virat wrote a letter to his 15-year-old self. It made fascinating reading. He apologised for not telling his younger self all the things life had in store for him, but insisted that not knowing what was coming would make "every surprise sweet, every challenge thrilling and every disappointment an opportunity to learn." He assured his younger self that the journey he will go on is "SUPER!"

"You need to be ready for each and every opportunity that comes your way. Grab it when it comes. And never take what you have for granted. You will fail. Everyone does.

Just promise yourself that you'll never forget to rise. And if at first you don't, try again."

Virat finished his letter with:

"Finally, just follow your heart, chase your dreams, be kind, and show the world how dreaming big makes all the difference. Be you.

Make every day Super!"

Virat couldn't resist adding a final cheeky line about the sacrifices he had made to become a fit, lean, world class run-scoring machine . . .

"And . . . savour those parathas, buddy! They'll become quite a luxury in years to come . . . ☺"

Virat Kohli Fact File

(as of January 2024)

Born: 05/11/1988, Delhi, India

Tests
113 matches
8,848 runs, 111 catches
29 hundreds, 30 fifties
Batting average: 49.15

ODIs
292 matches
13,848 runs, 5 wickets, 151 catches
50 hundreds, 72 fifties
Batting average: 58.67

T20 Internationals
115 matches
4,008 runs, 4 wickets, 50 catches
1 hundred, 37 fifties
Batting average: 52.73

Turn the page for a sample of

Amazing Cricket Stars – Ben Stokes

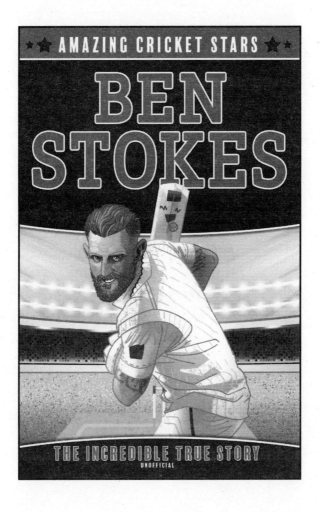

★ CHAPTER 1 ★

By the Barest of Margins

Four hard years of work, seven weeks of competition, 99.5 overs of tough cricket on the day and it all came down to this: 14 July, in front of a packed crowd at Lord's Cricket Ground in London, Ben Stokes faced the final ball of the 2019 ICC World Cup Final and the whole of England – as well as New Zealand – held its breath.

The previous ball had seen Adil Rashid lose his wicket: run out as he and Ben had strived to add two to the score. Ben's heart was still thumping from sprinting those runs . . . and from the hugeness of the occasion. England were

241–9, needing two runs to win, one to tie and with only one wicket left. Any mistake could cost the match and the last man in was Mark Wood – 'Woody' – the lovable, lightning-fast bowler who was also Ben's pal and teammate at Durham.

Each team in a Cricket World Cup One Day International (ODI) match gets 50 overs to compile as big a score as possible or chase down their opponent's total to win. The World Cup was first held in 1975 and England had never been champions, although they had come desperately close, losing in the final three times.

"Come on England!"

Ben had been in good form throughout the tournament. He'd struck 89 versus South Africa in England's opening game, and added scores of 79 (v India), 82 (v Sri Lanka) and 89 again (v Australia). He didn't bat in the semi-final as England trounced their oldest cricketing rival, Australia, by reaching their target of 223 with more than 17 overs to spare – an absolute thrashing. How England loved knocking their old foe out with ease!

But the final was proving to be a much tighter, nerve-jangling contest.

In front of almost 30,000 fans, England had bowled well to keep New Zealand's score down to 241, but they'd struggled in their run chase on a sticky pitch. They were 86–4 until hard-hitting Jos Buttler and Ben put on a stellar partnership of 110 runs. But then Jos fell, skying a ball high into the air for New Zealand quick bowler Tim Southee to catch. Chris Woakes, Liam Plunkett and Jofra Archer all followed. It had been left to Ben to score the remaining runs as evening loomed and the crowd worked itself into a frenzy.

Fifteen runs were still needed off the last over, to be bowled by the Kiwis' premier fast bowler, Trent Boult. Ben spoke to his batting partner, Adil Rashid. "I need to take all six balls – so no running, unless we can get two." Adil nodded and settled nervously at the non-striker's end. Could Stokesy do it?

49.1: Ben strikes the ball but sees it is heading to a New Zealand fielder. He decides not to run so he can keep the strike and face the next ball.

49.2: Trent bowls a good delivery which Ben gets his bat on but fails to score from. Now, it's 15 runs off just four balls . . . and the pressure is mounting.

49.3: Down goes Ben on one knee: a slog-sweep, and up, up and away flies the ball. It sails high over the midwicket boundary. The crowd roars. SIX!

49.4: Ben pushes the ball, the pair run two but as the throw is returned, it hits

Ben's outstretched bat and cannons off to the boundary. Ben apologises – he knew nothing about it as the ball had been thrown from behind him – but four is still added to the two that he and Adil ran. ANOTHER SIX!

49.5: Again, Ben and Adil go for two, but this time Adil is run out. Nooo!

49.6: The final ball. Ben drives it low on the leg side, mindful of not getting out Caught and losing England the game. He and Woody sprint for their lives . . . the pair manage one run to level the scores, but Jimmy Neesham had gathered the ball and hurled it towards Trent Boult who was lurking by the stumps. Woody, knowing he was short, desperately hurled himself forward

into a full-length dive . . . but Trent
had gathered the ball and clattered
the stumps.

OUT! The game was tied.

Ben was furious and kicked his bat 10 metres
away with frustration. Woody picked himself
up and ran up to him. "Mate, you've been
absolutely fantastic. You've given us a chance of
winning." But Ben felt he'd let the team down.

One Day International Cricket was
now entering uncharted territory. For the first
time in 4,129 ODI matches, a game would
be decided by a Super Over. Each team
could pick any pair of batters to face six balls.
Whoever scores the most runs, wins. England
were to bat first.

Ben and Woody returned to an England
dressing room in chaos. Players were scrabbling
for their kit and hotly debating what should be
done. Ben needed a moment to regain focus.

Adrenaline surged through him. He needed to get a calm head, so he took himself off into the showers for five minutes.

England's captain, Eoin Morgan, remained ice-cool though. He wanted a left-hander and a right-hander to bat and chose Jos Buttler and Ben. Even though he suggested Jason Roy instead of himself, Ben marched out with Jos. He would do whatever the captain demanded and the team wanted.

The pair scored 15 runs, which felt a formidable total until Jimmy Neesham hit a six off Jofra Archer in New Zealand's reply. Suddenly, New Zealand needed just seven off four balls, then five off three, then just two off the final ball. Lord's fell silent.

The ground was half bathed in sunlight, half in shadow, as Jofra Archer hurtled in to bowl.

Martin Guptill hit the ball out towards deep midwicket as Jason Roy sped in from the boundary to field.

J-Roy hurled the ball towards Jos Buttler, England's wicketkeeper, as the New Zealand batters ran hard . . .

As Jos gathered and smashed the stumps with the ball, TV commentator Ian Smith roared, *"ENGLAND HAVE WON THE WORLD CUP! BY THE BAREST OF MARGINS! BY THE BAREST OF ALL MARGINS!"*

There was nothing between the two teams. Both had scored 241 off 50 overs and then 15 off their Super Over, but the winner was decided by the team who had scored the most boundaries – New Zealand had struck 17, England, 26, seven of which were Ben's.

Ben sprinted across the ground to join a gaggle of his teammates. Everyone was going wild.

England had won the Cricket World Cup for the first time in front of a spellbound audience. The game was considered the most exciting in Cricket World Cup history and New Zealand-born Ben was awarded Man of the Match.

Hours later, England's dressing room was rowdy and packed with players, their families and the trophy. They only left when Lord's closed down at midnight, filling the air with songs and cheers.

"Brilliant, Stokesy!"

"Well played, Jofra!"

"We are the Champions!"

"*Allez! Allez! Allez!*"

"It's coming! Cricket's coming home!"

The England players marvelled at the game and Ben in their post-match interviews.

"I thought I'd seen everything in cricket, but that game was just ridiculous," chuckled Jos Buttler.

Joe Root, Ben's great mate on the team, singled him out. "It's almost written in the stars for Ben. Everything he's gone through – I can't be more proud and pleased for him."

The captain, Eoin Morgan, called him, "almost superhuman".

Ben, though, wasn't going to let all the praise get to his head and recalled the words he had spoken quietly to Jofra just before the young pace bowler bowled the Super Over.

"Everyone believes in you. Whatever happens here – this isn't going to define your career."

Ben knew only too well how cricket produced crushing lows as well as incredible highs, and how what you learned from the lows can help improve you as a cricketer. In Ben's case, he only had to think back three years to a previous World Cup Final . . .

★ CHAPTER 2 ★

World Cup Low

"Typical Rooty, scampering quick singles,"
thought Ben on the balcony as his mate,
Joe Root, top scored for England with 54.
Ben had only contributed 13 runs before
a good length ball from West Indian quick
Dwayne Bravo had smashed into his stumps.

The game was the ICC World Twenty20 Final
in 2016. England had cruised to the final with
Joe Root shining throughout. Now, in front of
66,000 fans at Eden Gardens in Kolkata, Ben
and the rest of the team had the chance to
go for glory and win a major competition.

England only managed a modest total of

155 in warm, sticky conditions. The Eden Gardens pitch was pretty flat and good for batting, so it would need something special from Ben and the rest of the bowlers and fielders to stop the West Indies from passing England's total.

It came in the second over from their surprising skipper, Eoin Morgan. He brought on Joe to bowl. "Why not Moeen Ali?" Ben had thought as he trotted to field at mid-on. Seconds later, the ball flew gently straight into Ben's hands. Joe had taken a wicket with his first ball! "Morgs, you genius," Ben cheered as the team huddled together.

Next in to bat was Chris Gayle – the 'Universe Boss' – and one of the deadliest T20 hitters in the game. To prove the point, Gayle pummelled the first ball he faced for a powerful four.

Joe's next ball was also smashed high, but this time towards the long on boundary . . . where Ben was now fielding. He moved sharply and took a great catch. Two down in two overs. And then David Willey reduced the Windies to 11–3 in the next over. Brilliant!

Marlon Samuels rebuilt the innings with a great knock of 85, but with just one over to go the West Indies needed 19 runs, and their batters would be facing Ben.

Eoin gave Ben a look. Both felt confident as Ben had bowled the last over in the previous two matches for England and they'd gone really well.

In the first game, Sri Lanka had needed 15 runs to win with their dangerous all-rounder, Angelo Mathews, at the crease. Ben managed to bowl six near-perfect deliveries right at Angelo's feet, making it impossible to hit a big boundary shot. Ben's over cost just four runs. England were through to the semis!

END OF SAMPLE

About the Author

CLIVE GIFFORD is an award-winning author of more than 200 books, including the official guide to the ICC Cricket World Cup 2019. His books have won the Blue Peter Children's Book Award, the Royal Society Young People's Book Prize, the School Library Association's Information Book Award and Smithsonian Museum's Notable Books For Children. Clive lives in Manchester within a short walk of Lancashire's Old Trafford cricket ground.

Read more sports books from Red Shed!

Amazing Cricket Stars

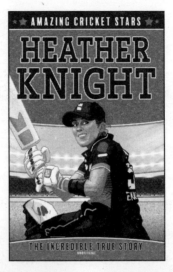

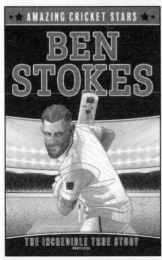

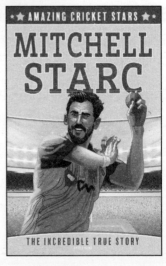

Incredible Sports Stories

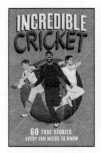   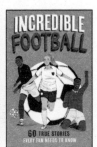

Amazing Football Facts

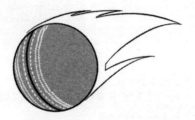